Riding to the Rescue!

Rescue Helicopters

B.J. Best

Cavendish
Square
New York

Published in 2018 by Cavendish Square Publishing, LLC
243 5th Avenue, Suite 136, New York, NY 10016

Library of Congress Cataloging-in-Publication Data

Names: Best, B. J., 1976- author.
Title: Rescue helicopters / B.J. Best.
Description: New York : Cavendish Square Publishing, [2018] | Series: Riding to the rescue! | Includes index.
Identifiers: LCCN 2016052304 (print) | LCCN 2016054168 (ebook) | ISBN 9781502625748 (pbk.) | ISBN 9781502625588 (6 pack) | ISBN 9781502625700 (library bound) | ISBN 9781502625649 (E-book)
Subjects: LCSH: Helicopters in search and rescue operations--Juvenile literature.
Classification: LCC TL553.8 .B47 2018 (print) | LCC TL553.8 (ebook) | DDC 363.34/810284--dc23
LC record available at https://lccn.loc.gov/2016052304

The photographs in this book are used by permission and through the courtesy of:
Cover Ashley Cooper/Corbis Documentary/Getty Images Entertainment/Getty Images; p. 5 Daxiao Productions/Shutterstock; p. 7 Jeff J Mitchell/Staff/Getty Images News/Getty Images Entertainment/Getty Images; p. 9 Richard Wayman/Alamy Stock Photo; p. 11 Blickwinkel/Alamy Stock Photo; p. 13 Alex Brylov/Shutterstock; p. 15 Hernis/Alamy Stock Photo; p. 17 Nightman1965/Shutterstock; p. 19 Ivan Cholakov/Shutterstock; p. 21 Monkey Business Images/Shutterstock.

Printed in the United States of America

Contents

A **hiker** is lost on a mountain!

The hiker needs help!

5

A rescue helicopter will help.

It can fly to places that are hard to reach.

The helicopter will find the hiker.

Rescue helicopters are big.

They need power.

They need space.

They have a **crew** who
will help.

A **rescuer** comes out of the helicopter.

The rescuer is on a rope.

The rescuer is held by a **harness**.

11

The rescuer finds the hiker.

They go up the rope together.

The helicopter flies away.

Sometimes a boat can sink.

A person can be lost at sea.

15

The rescue helicopter flies over the sea.

It is windy.

There are waves. The **pilot** flies safely.

17

The rescuer comes down.

The rescuer saves the person in the water.

They go up together.

19

Rescue helicopters go to many places.

The rescuers save lives.

They are heroes!

21

New Words

crew (CROO) People who work on a helicopter.

harness (HAR-ness) Something that holds a person.

hiker (HIKE-er) Someone who walks.

pilot (PIE-lut) The person who flies a helicopter.

rescuer (RESS-kyoo-er) Someone who rescues.

Index

23

About the Author

B.J. Best lives in Wisconsin with his wife and son. He has written several other books for children. He has hiked on mountains but has never needed to be rescued.

About BOOKWORMS

Bookworms help independent readers gain reading confidence through high-frequency words, simple sentences, and strong picture/text support. Each book explores a concept that helps children relate what they read to the world they live in.